MW00878336

IMMIGRATING TO ISRAEL

BY

BRUCE A. HURWITZ, PH.D.

WWW.HSSTAFFING.COM

Library of Congress Cataloguing-in-Publication Data

Hurwitz, Bruce A.

Immigrating to Israel / Bruce A. Hurwitz – 1st ed.

ISBN: 9781728621562

To all those who graciously helped make my immigration to Israel a success.

TABLE OF CONTENTS

FORWARD

MANY years ago, in a previous life, I was a fundraiser for a Jewish Federation. In that capacity, I attended a conference on Planned Giving at Disneyland. There was a restaurant at the hotel which, throughout the day, featured a different Disney character in the lobby.

One morning I went into the restaurant to see Pluto, a personal favorite of mine. I was the only man there. The other patrons were mothers with their children.

One little boy asked his mother, "Is that really Pluto or is it a man in a costume?"

"It's really Pluto," she assured him.

"Really?" he asked.

"Yes, it's really Pluto."

He then looked around, saw me and approached. He was very polite.

"Excuse me, sir."

"Yes."

"Is that really Pluto or is it a man in a costume?"

His mother and I looked at each other. She had a confused expression on her face. I probably did as well. Silently, we were both asking the same question.

"It's really Pluto," I told him.

He thanked me and returned to his mother.

She wasn't exactly angry; more perplexed than anything else.

"Why did you ask that man if it was really Pluto? I told you it was."

Without missing a beat he said, "Because Daddy told me men don't lie!"

It took us all a couple of seconds to figure it out, but all the mothers, including his, smiled and chuckled, as did I.

I moved to Israel in 1977 and remained until 1990. I lived in the country for 13 years and three months. This book is based on my experiences in Israel and, in some of cases, after my return. It is the truth, the whole truth and nothing but the truth, with one caveat. Even though some 40 years have passed, and the people involved have moved on, hopefully to bigger and better, I have changed identifying characteristics so no one can say they know about whom I am writing. In a couple of cases I went further, putting myself in a story of which I was not involved (in which case I do have first-hand knowledge of what happened) or replacing myself with someone else. If you will, I have adopted the *Dragnet* definition of truth – the names have been changed to protect the innocent, or guilty, as the case may be.

Which brings me back to my friend Pluto. In these pages Pluto is really a man in a costume. No one has ever written a book like this before. It is the truth about the motivation of Americans and Canadians to immigrate to Israel. If you don't want to know that Pluto is a man in a costume, don't read it! If you want to save your relationship with your children, and possibly their lives, continue reading.

They say, "There is no such thing as bad children, only good children behaving badly." That may or may not be true. But there are certainly bad parents. You will meet many in the following pages. Here's an example which motivated me to put fingers to keyboard – which does not sound nearly as good as "pen to paper."

Recently I was in a kosher restaurant. I was seated at a table next to a young woman and her mother. It was heartbreaking. Everything the mother said to her daughter, a senior in high school, was a backhanded compliment:

You have such a beautiful face. Why do you wear your hair like that?

You're such a beautiful girl. Why don't you have a date to the dance?

But what really got me was when the waitress came over to take their orders. The mother said,

She'll have the mixed vegetables, not the fries. She has to watch her weight!

I was sitting beside the mother, across from the daughter. I saw the look of embarrassment and humiliation on her face. I looked at her, smiled and asked, “So, which Israeli universities have you applied to?” As she looked at me in amazement, her mother turned to me and asked, “How did you know she wants to go to Israel?”

Well, this book is about how I knew. And one more word of warning, I tell it like it is and do not mince my words. There are times when one needs to be subtle. This is not one of them. My goal is to get parents to change and children to find courage. You can’t do that with subtlety!

Many people will be offended by what I have written. So let me answer my critics now, to get it out of the way: I do not care! If a thousand people burn me in effigy, and one person calls or emails to thank me for having gotten their parents to change their behavior, it will be worth it. If a thousand people burn me in effigy, and one person calls or emails to thank me for having given them the courage to stand up for themselves, lay down the law, and not have to leave their country and friends, it will be worth it. I do not care that parents will no longer be able to brag about having children living in Israel. I do not care that parents will no longer be able to play the martyr because they have children living in Israel. All I care about are the children.

Bruce Hurwitz

INTRODUCTION

AS I said, I lived in Israel for 13 years. I served in the Army for a year and a half. I received my bachelor's, master's and doctorate from the Hebrew University. I am proud of every one of the accomplishments I had in Israel. It was a great experience. That said, it should never have happened.

In Israel, in the late '70s, there was a popular joke. It went something like this:

A man is lying on his bed in the hospital. The Angel of Death arrives.

"I have good news and bad news."

"Give me the bad news first."

"You are going to die."

"So, what's the good news?"

"You get to decide if you go to Heaven or Hell."

"Great!"

"Let me show you each so you'll be able to make an informed decision."

Poof! The man is in Hell. It's hot. It's humid. There's hard work.

Poof! The man is in Heaven. Everything is idyllic. The weather is perfect. There's no work. There are no troubles. Anything you want you instantly receive.

Poof! Back in the hospital.

"So," asked the Angel, "Heaven was truly beautiful, but boring. In Hell there was hard work, but there was commiseration along with the misery. You had what to do and were not alone. I choose Hell!"

Poof, he's back in Hell. Only this time he is being chased by a devil with a pitchfork and fire is all around him.

The man yells at the Angel, "This is not the place you showed me!"

The Angel replies, "Yes, it is. But the last time you were here you were a tourist!"

I had been to Israel a few times prior to immigrating in '77. The first was for my *bar mitzvah* in '71. Then I was back about every two years. I liked it. I liked the way I was treated. I liked what I saw. I liked the people.

Of course, I did not speak the language, nor did I understand the culture. I was seeing the country as a tourist. Reality, as I would later discover, was quite different.

But this is not a book about the faults of Israeli society. It's a book about motivation. What causes young people from Canada and the United States to move to Israel? That is the topic of this book.

I can hear what you are thinking. *You moved four decades ago. How are your experiences relevant today?*

Well, the story I related about the mother and daughter in the restaurant shows that things have not changed. And you will be reading others which are more current, one very current.

******

I am blessed, or cursed, with the courage of my convictions. I am very conservative. I believe that there are two fundamental principles that can never be violated: First, personal responsibility. If you did it, it's on you. Period. Second, the dignity of the individual. People must always be treated with respect. Period.

That is why, when a parent humiliates a child, and the child, even a decade or more later, moves to Israel to get away from them and to milk them for as much money as possible, I have no problem with it. And if, instead of money, they choose to abandon them and deny any responsibility for, or recognition to, their parents, more power to them.

The conviction I have relevant to immigration to Israel is that *all* Americans and Canadians who *move* to Israel do so because of varying degrees of hatred toward their parents or other first-degree relatives. All. No exceptions. Based on my experience, no American or Canadian who I met or heard about moved to Israel for anything other than the desire – really the need – to place an ocean and continent between them and "family." Religious, secular; liberal, conservative. It made no difference. *All* moved to get away from family.

Now let me clarify something. I said "move." There are plenty of Americans and Canadians who go to Israel to study. They do not hate their relatives; they want a good education. There are those who move for a limited time for work. They too do not hate their relatives. But any American or Canadian who *moves* to Israel permanently, does so to get away from family. That is my sincere belief.

Now in the past, I don't know if this is still possible, some people moved to establish themselves as "Israel experts" so they could return home to work for Jewish organizations. They went through the motions of moving, but had no intention of staying. To coin a phrase, when the going got tough, they got going. One example will suffice.

Years after I returned from Israel, I was working with a fellow for whom I developed an immediate dislike. (For the record, the feeling was mutual.) He was always talking about his years in Israel on a *kibbutz* – a collective farm. Something did not smell right. Finally, as he was going on and on in a meeting about how great he had been in Israel, I finally had had enough:

How long did you live in Israel?

Three years.

(On hearing that, I knew what was coming. Almost to the day, after I had been in Israel for three years, I received a letter from the Ministry of the Interior asking me if I wanted to renew my Student visa. I did. Two years later, the choice was citizenship or Permanent Resident status.)

What was your status?

I was an Immigrant.

Did you serve in the Army?

No.

Well, after three years the Immigrant visa expires and you have to either become a Permanent Resident or a citizen. What did you do?

My girlfriend wanted to get married but did not want to live in Israel.

Well, if you entered the country on an Immigrant visa you received financial benefits. Did you have to repay the money to the State?

No and I intended to return. My parents wanted me to come back because my mother was sick.

So first it was his girlfriend. Literally, a few seconds later it was his mother. What probably happened was that he did not want to enlist in the Army which he would have had to do either as a citizen or Permanent Resident. Additionally, his parents probably told him that the gravy train was ending, they would cut him off; he had to get a real job, or come home. No more playing pioneer on a *kibbutz*. He returned home.

After everyone realized what he really was all about, he never spoke about his time in Israel again – at least not around me!

*****

I've debated this so often that I know what you are thinking. *How many Americans and Canadians could you have known to make it possible for you to draw such an all-encompassing conclusion that ALL Americans and Canadians move to Israel to get away from their parents or relatives?*

When I was in high school, the two most important classes I took were typing (who knew?) and public speaking. When I arrived at the Hebrew University, I immediately applied for a job in the Economics Library as a typist. From there, I got a job at what was then called the "School for Overseas Students." I worked there for five years, on and off. My first job was in Admissions and my last was as Dormitory and Tuition Clerk. Over the years, I interacted with thousands of students.

The non-North Americans who had come to the university as part of their immigration did so to get away from anti-Semitism. The exceptions were those coming from Australia (I don't remember any students from New Zealand) and southern Africa. The Aussies wanted to be closer to the rest of the world and the South Africans and (I think there were a few) Rhodesians wanted to get away from Apartheid.

The largest cohort of students was from North America. In other words, each year I interacted with hundreds of Americans and Canadians at the university and also, indirectly, through my contacts at the Association of Americans and Canadians in Israel which helped North American immigrants. (A friend worked there and she was always sharing stories with me about her clients. She could commiserate with them because, like them, she too hated her parents. That was why she was so good at her job. She understood what they were going through because she had experienced the same things herself.)

Sorry, but my conclusion is not based on a few friends. It is based on the experiences of hundreds of people all of whom basically had the same story:

Their parents had humiliated and embarrassed them as children. They, the children, wanted to be rid of their parents. But they did not want to lose their financial support. Israel was the answer. The parents would brag about how their child was living in Israel. They would play the martyr and pay for the privilege.

Now there are some exceptions:

Many adults move to Israel for employment. This is not a short-term decision. They are immigrating. They uproot their children because they have failed in their chosen profession at home and believe they will be more successful in Israel. But, even in these cases, it's a way to get increased financial support from their parents – *for the grandkids!*

And then there are the married couples. Here's one example:

Sarah hated her parents. Passionately. I never knew what they had done to her; her husband, my friend, told me not to ask and to never mention them. Whatever it was, it was so bad that, as a youth, every year she would sign-up for a "summer in Israel" program. From the time of her *bat mitzvah*, aged 12, she spent every summer in Israel preparing her parents for her eventual move.

Her parents would always beam to their friends about their daughter spending her summers doing this, that or the other thing in Israel. It was all a setup. Once she completed her undergraduate degree, she announced she would go to university in Israel to continue her studies. Her parents could not possibly object. For a decade they had been singing her praises. How could they stand in her way now? And when she decided to immigrate, they had no choice but to pay.

And pay they did. But it did not matter because they had money. As her husband told me, she did not want to wait for her inheritance; she wanted to get it *now*. And the fact that it infuriated her siblings, who knew what she was doing, was icing on the cake.

Which brings me to her husband. He did not hate his parents; he was ambivalent toward them. They were lower middle class. They would save during the year to send him to a private Jewish summer camp. Instead of appreciating their efforts, instead of being grateful, he resented the fact that he did not have what the "rich kids" had. (In my own defense, as I got to know him better, the friendship ended. Gradually, I became closer to his wife and kids. A good person he was not. Ironically, his children eventually left Israel. Apparently, in some cases, it works both ways! More on that in a bit.)

In any event, he wanted money and the only way he could get it was through marriage. So while studying for his undergraduate degree, he met Sarah. She made it clear that she planned on getting her graduate degree in Israel and move there. He was fine with that.

She moved to Israel out of hatred for her parents. He moved to Israel because he wanted a rich wife. So, if it makes you feel better, not *every* American and Canadian moves to Israel out of hatred, or dislike, of their parents. Sometimes the hatred is by marriage!

*****

One day, in the early '80s, I was riding in the car with friends, a married couple. He was Brazilian; she was Russian. I was talking to their daughter-in-law. She asked me why I had moved to Israel. I told her, "Like all Americans and Canadians, I wanted to get as far away from my relatives as possible."

Her mother-in-law took exception to what I had said. (I rightly chose to tone it down and did not use the word "hatred." I had learned that Israelis and non-North American immigrants simply did not understand and would become very agitated and defensive hearing "hatred." Diplomacy was the best course of action.) She was adamant that that was not the case. As far as she was concerned, I was unique.

I dropped it. There was no point in arguing. But when, a few minutes later, I was alone with the daughter-in-law, she told me that her husband's business partner was American and that he had told her that he had immigrated to Israel because he hated his parents.

Is there a theoretical possibility that today there are Americans and Canadians moving to Israel for reasons other than hatred of their parents? Yes. Do I believe that it is more than theoretical? No.

Perhaps this incident will help:

When I was the Dormitory and Tuition Clerk, I was responsible for student housing. Moving Day was hell on earth. Hundreds of students moving out of their summer dorms into new quarters, all with some complaint.

One exceptionally attractive student showed up with a unique (for the day) problem. There was an Israeli who would not leave her alone. He was at that moment following (stalking?) her. She asked if I minded if she told him off in my office. She wanted a witness and was a bit afraid as she did not know how he would react.

Naturally, I had no problem helping. I knew her fear was real, if unjustified. I did not believe for a moment that she was in physical danger. I figured he was just interested in the coveted visa to the States. If not her, he'd find someone else. I saw it every day.

A minute or two later the Israeli barged in. She told him to leave her alone. I told him to get out of the office. It did not help. Then she said, "Why would I move to Israel? I don't hate my parents!" On hearing that, he turned on his heels and left. She plopped down on a chair and we both laughed. Then I told her to look outside. I could not see what was happening, but I knew. Sure enough, he was hitting on another American girl!

I kept notes on the stories behind Americans and Canadians moving to Israel. This book is based on those notes. They are in no particular order, although the first happened about a year ago and shows that, as much as things change, they remain the same.

And remember, "the names have been changed to protect the innocent," so don't try to identify the people involved. You can't. You will guess wrong. Just keep in mind the motivations of the children and the actions of the parents. If you are a parent, don't do what these parents did. If you are a child, you are not alone. As for whether or not you should move to Israel, it is not for me to say. You are making an irrational decision which, ironically, may be rational. But keep in mind the story I am about to tell. It may help you.

I

IT is sometimes difficult to get time zones straight. I really can't complain. When I was leaving Israel I called a friend in Vancouver at 3:00 in the morning, his time. I don't think he ever forgave me!

So when, a year or so ago, my phone rang at some ungodly hour, I could not really chastise my friend, who was in Israel, too much, especially since he was trying to save a life – two lives actually.

A close friend of his was getting married. He had known her since kindergarten. This was no "bribe and brand" engagement. They were serious. They were negotiating a pre-nup. They were focused on marriage, not parties and presents.

He told me she was a good person with a mother who was truly human garbage. Her father always sided with her, the mother, making excuses for her behavior. She hated her mother and despised her father.

He asked me to call her because she was thinking that the only solution to her problem was to move to Israel. As he put it, “She doesn’t deserve it!”

He gave me her number and told me to wait a day before I called, so he could prepare her.

When we spoke I asked her why she was getting married. She had only the most positive things to say about her fiancé. She was not marrying him to hurt or get away from her parents (which, as you will read, happens). He was a quality person and she wanted him to be her husband and the father of her children.

Then I asked her about Israel. She said she had to get away from her mother or she would kill her. She could not allow her to be near her children, which she hoped to have. I suggested moving to a non-grandparents’ rights state, such as Rhode Island. She said she had considered that, but laws change. I told her that I thought Israel recognized grandparents’ rights. She said it did not matter. In Israel she would be in control, not her mother.

Then I asked what had happened most recently. She explained that her mother was interfering with the pre-nup negotiations and was demanding that she discuss with her the wedding reception. (Classic putting the cart before the horse.) If she was interfering now, she knew she would be interfering with the marriage and the raising of the children.

I then asked her to describe what happens when she argues with her mother. She told me that her mother immediately storms out of the room, calls their rabbi and the rabbi calls and pressures her to give in to her mother's demands, which she always does.

Now my focus changed to the rabbi. I asked her to tell me about him. She said that he had two sons and that they both had moved to Israel. That was all I needed to hear.

At that point I ended the conversation. As I noted previous, I have the courage of my convictions. If you are American or Canadian and live in Israel, you hate your parents. I now knew what I needed to do.

I told her not to worry. All I needed was the address in Israel of the rabbi's sons. She was concerned about how she would get it. I told her to simply call the rabbi explaining that she was thinking of moving to, or even just visiting, Israel and wanted to write them. She did and he gladly provided their addresses. (They lived in separate apartments in the same city).

When she emailed me the addresses, I forwarded the email to our mutual friend in Israel. He then got to work. It turned out that the brothers would meet every Friday at a café. He had two women go to the café, sit near them, and start talking about why they had moved to Israel. The brothers joined the conversation and provided their reasons for having immigrated.

With that information in hand, I called the bride-to-be and told her to tell her mother that she and her groom-to-be would be coming over that evening to discuss their marriage and wedding. She explained that she had a commitment but would be able to do it the following evening.

That was fine. I told her I would call the rabbi and set everything up. I assured her that when her mother called him crying, he would tell her to mind her own business.

I phoned the rabbi and introduced myself. I explained that the following evening the bride and groom would be meeting with her mother and she would be laying down the law. She would make it clear that the mother's opinion was neither requested nor required about the pre-nup, nor was her consent about or, for that matter, presence at, the marriage ceremony or reception. The happy couple was going to do what they wanted. If the mother did not like it, she did not have to attend the wedding. They had agreed to the terms of the pre-nup and those terms were none of the mother's business. And, if she caused any problems, they would move to Israel.

I then told the rabbi that, as she always did, the mother would call him so he could call and pressure the daughter. Only this time, I said, he would not side with the mother but with the daughter and make it clear that her interference, and his involvement, were over.

He then politely interrupted me and I let him say his peace. When he was finished lecturing me on the Fifth (according to the Hebrew Bible, for my non-Jewish readers) Commandment, I continued.

If you do not support the daughter then at this Saturday's service, I told him, she would make an announcement. She would inform the congregation that on such-and-such a date she would be getting married and that shortly thereafter she and her husband would be moving to Israel. She would then explain that "like all Americans who move to Israel, I am moving to get as far away from my parents as humanly possible. While the rabbi's sons left because he and his wife had publicly embarrassed them, we will be leaving because my mother is constantly interfering in my life and my father isn't man enough to do anything about it. I will not have them near my children."

Then I asked the rabbi if it was true that he had based a sermon on his son's first date, which had not gone well, and that his wife, on their other son's *bar mitzvah*, had teased him after she had spilled juice on his trousers. He did not reply.

Children remember humiliation. I started hating my parents on my eighth birthday. The rabbi's sons started hating him and their mother when they were teenagers. Despite the passage of time, the hatred remains and the humiliation is never forgotten and rarely forgiven.

The next day, as predicted, after her daughter laid down the law, her mother went storming out of the room and called the rabbi. She returned a few minutes later white as a ghost. The rabbi had told her to mind her own business and not to call him anymore. And then a prediction I made came true:

I had warned the daughter that after the rabbi had played his part in this tragedy, her mother would fake a heart attack. I said that that was standard operating procedure. I told her to ask her mother if she wanted her to call an ambulance and, before she had a change to answer, to nonchalantly tell her fiancé that, according to Jewish law, they would have to wait 90 days to get married following her mother's death. (I remembered reading that somewhere.) But, I told her to add, they could have a civil marriage right away.

Surprisingly, her mother's chest pains instantly vanished, as did the daughter's need to move to Israel.

II

PURIM is a fun holiday. It commemorates the Jews victory over Haman, the Persian ruler who planned to exterminate them. (Sound familiar? Some things just don't change!) Children dress up in costumes and a good time is had by all. With one exception.

Mark was the nicest person you would ever want to meet. He was a great colleague and friend. Except when *Purim* came around. He would get nervous. *Very* nervous. He knew what was coming.

Purim is a month before Passover. Every year his parents would send him a letter (this was in the days before the Internet, when dinosaurs roamed the Earth) wishing him a happy holiday and asking, telling, him to book a hotel for them for the holiday and instructing him to join them.

He hated them. He hated the idea of their coming to Israel. He would stress out before they arrived, be inconsolable when they were there, and take weeks to recover from the ordeal.

I had advised him that the best thing he could do was simply to tell them to go to hell and leave him alone. He no longer needed their money, so why bother?

Then one year it happened. The letter arrived only this time it was different. They informed him that they had decided to move to Israel and would be arriving a week before Passover.

He was totally distraught. He called them and begged them not to come. He told them that they did not understand Israel. They did not speak the language. They did not understand the culture. It was a foreign country in every respect of the word.

His mother got on the phone and told him that she understood that he wanted to lead his own life. They would not live in Jerusalem. They wanted to live in Netanya. He would not even know they were in the country.

He begged. He pleaded. To no avail.

On the accursed day, I went with him to the airport to pick them up. Going to Netanya, I would drive his car (which was about to become mine) and he would drive the rental which he had reserved at the airport for his parents.

When we arrived at the apartment, he showed them around. The kitchen was fully stocked. There was bedding, towels and everything else. He had also written a guide for them clearly indicating how to get to the lawyer, the health clinic, the local branch of the Association of Americans and Canadians in Israel, the bank, everything. They had nothing to complain about but his mother, instead of thanking him, complained about the coffee!

On hearing her complaint and lack of appreciation, Mark smiled and sighed a sigh of relief. His parents were ungrateful. He had made the right decision.

As she was sipping her substandard coffee, I told Mark that we had to get going or he would miss his flight. His parents asked, "What flight?"

Then all the hatred came flowing out. It may have been only a few minutes but if felt a lot longer. He let them know exactly what he thought of them. He reminded them of all the humiliations.

When he was finished his mother said, "But we moved her to be with you!" To which he responded, "But you told me the exact opposite."

Then they asked where he was moving. He refused to tell them. He made it clear he was starting a new life and he never wanted to see or hear from them again. And he made it equally clear that no one, myself included, knew where he was going.

As we drove to the airport he started to cry. I knew those tears. I had seen them before. They were tears of joy. The nightmare was over. He could now live his life.

III

I had only been back in the States for a few months. A close friend, Steve, was getting married. Allow me to explain:

There are a few different approaches to moving to Israel. The first is simply to put distance between you and your parents and to get as much money out of them as possible. That's the simplest. That measure of revenge (the topic of the Afterword) is usually enough for most. Then, after a few years, you gradually transform the relationship to an exchange of greeting cards, corresponding to a decrease in the need for financial support.

The next stage of revenge deals with marriage and children. Some make the ultimate sacrifice and, if they have no siblings, kill off the family line by never marrying or having children which, as you will read, was the route I chose to take.

Others, prior to immigrating to Israel, become involved with a gentile and threaten to marry them if their parents don't back off. If that doesn't work, then they move to Israel.

I can remember one girl, who had actually moved to Israel, who was so fed up with her parents interfering in her life – the distance had made no difference – that she returned to the States, ostensibly permanently but, in reality, only for a few months. She had a plan. Her parents' money was no longer required, only their silence and absence!

She had a friend arrange for her to meet a black man. They went on a few dates. When she brought him home, her parents were horrified. She then produced an unsigned marriage license. She was not bluffing. She read them the Riot Act and gave them a choice, no more interference or "black grandbabies." They never bothered her again.

Probably the largest cohort marries Israelis. But they choose wisely. They marry Israelis who speak little or no English and whose parents were born in non-English speaking, especially Arab, countries. In other words, their parents would not be able to communicate with their spouse or in-laws. No communication means little to no interference.

Steve had found himself a gorgeous Yemenite woman. She was not a university graduate. She spoke very little English. Her parents were good, decent people and, by Western standards, very primitive. She would make a good wife and mother. The only thing lacking would be intellectual stimulation.

When Steve's parents visited him in Israel, he introduced them to his then-girlfriend and her parents. They were distraught. It was great! They could not communicate with them. It was perfect!

Besides the lack of communication, they were very uncomfortable with the fact that she, and her parents, were religious. While they were acquainted with some aspects of Jewish orthodoxy, the Sephardic tradition was totally foreign to them. In other words, they did not have a clue what was going on.

When Steve told them that he was planning on asking her to marry him, they offered money to end the relationship. They invited him to return to Canada promising to leave him alone. (Funny how they figured out why he had moved to Israel!) He would not give in. He knew they were lying. We had all heard that story too many times. They would be married.

Of course, it would not be a marriage based on "love," whatever that means. If you will, he loved her but was not "in love" with her. It would be a marriage based on pure, unadulterated hatred. It would figuratively kill his parents, and if it were literal, so much the better. Either way, they would be irrelevancies in his life and, more importantly, in his children's.

Then fate stepped in. His parents were killed in a car accident. I got the call. I am a skeptic; I did not believe it – no one's luck is that good, so I demanded confirmation from five different sources: the Police, the local newspaper, the funeral home, the hospital and the rabbi.

When it was confirmed, I placed the call. Steve was actually at their engagement party. I told the owner of the catering hall where the celebration was taking place what had happened and asked him to have Steve come to the phone in a quiet room.

I gave him the news. After a few seconds I heard him say, "Thank God!" Then we discussed his next step. He had two options:

The first was to return to the party and announce the deaths. Everyone would understand that he had to return to Canada and postpone the wedding. We could find someone else for his girlfriend and transition in the kindest way possible. After all, she had done nothing wrong and there was no need, or desire, to hurt her. (She was not your standard Israeli just looking for a visa.) So he would return home and, over the course of a few months, communication would become sporadic and the chosen friend would take his place.

The second option was for him to return to the party, pick his girlfriend up and yell, "Yahoo! Now we really have something to celebrate. My parents died in a car crash. We won't have to raise our children in this damn country!"

Of course, the second option would result in the parents demanding that the engagement be cancelled and the girl being so confused that she would not object.

That said, she would likely be hurt and, again, that was something Steve wanted to avoid. (As noted, other Israelis had been engaged to Americans or Canadians simply for a chance to get a visa. When things fell apart, hurting them was never a problem.) Steve had the hall's owner ask a friend to join him.

A Canadian, he immediately understood. They discussed the two options and decided that instead of playing games and having Steve reduce contact with her over the course of time after returning home, it would be best to make a clean break of it. They chose a subtle version of Option Two. The friend liked Steve's girlfriend and agree to console her. When everything fell apart, his was the shoulder on which she cried. They eventually married. No harm, no foul.

IV

BECKY would cringe every time she heard the word "girl." That is what her father would call her, "Girl." He never used her name and she hated it. Her friends would tease her about it. (Some friends...) She pleaded with him to stop. He wouldn't. Her mother told her to forget about it. She never did.

It might seem like a little thing, but for a child, looking at things through a child's eyes, these slights are not little at all, they are huge. And as I already noted, they are never forgotten and are rarely forgiven.

Becky, who had moved to Israel, took a different approach to marriage than marrying an Israeli. She married a fellow American. Well, not quite. His parents were Americans who had immigrated to Israel in the early '50s, after the War of Independence, when American and Canadian Jews immigrated to Israel for ideological reasons. He was an Israeli by birth, American by citizenship and culture.

I was not happy with this marriage. I did not understand it. Her parents would be able to communicate with him and his parents. So what was the point? They would still make her life miserable.

Turned out, she wanted to move back to the States. She had reached the point where her hatred for her parents was no longer as great as her hatred for life in Israel. She certainly did not want to raise her children there. She had had enough and wanted out. Being married to an American would mean no visa problems.

But it still did not make any sense. I could not figure it out.

She knew I cared about her and was not trying to break up the engagement for any dishonorable motives. That's when she took me to dinner.

She told me that her fiancé was onboard with their moving to the States, as long as they moved to the east coast (her parents lived in California). I still did not get it.

She sat their smiling at the joke. "Think!" I ate. I drank. I thought. I just could not figure this one out. Then it dawned on me. I started to laugh.

Turnabout, really is, fair play. That I, of all people, had not seen this... Just goes to show, what's good for the goose *is* good for the gander! *He* wanted to leave Israel out of hatred for *his* parents. This was not about her at all!

V

AFTER 15 years, with the death of her father, Lynn decided to return to the States. She had had enough of Israel and was mature enough to be able to read the Riot Act to anyone interfering in her personal life.

Her first job back in the States was working for at a manufacturing company that was owned by an Orthodox Jew. Most of the senior staff were Jews, most of them observant. When she was interviewed, the boss asked her why she had moved to Israel. She responded, "Like all Americans, to get away from my parents."

The boss was not happy. He told her that there were some employees with children in Israel and she should not repeat that statement.

She didn't. But she did listen.

The boss was not a bad sort. His wife, on the other hand, was a nightmare. She took great pleasure in demeaning their one and only daughter, ridiculing here every chance she had because she could not keep a job.

One day, the daughter announced that she was moving to Israel. The boss knew what Lynn was thinking. He said nothing and neither did she. But their colleagues with children in Israel said a lot, behind closed doors, when the boss was not around.

They were convinced, and said so in no uncertain terms, that the daughter had moved to Israel to get away from her parents. What was so unbelievable was that they did not realize that their children had left to get away from them!

One of her colleagues would call her daughter in Israel every couple of days. She would talk to her and her grandchildren. It was impossible to tell to whom she was speaking because she spoke to *all* of them in baby talk. It was nauseating. She literally treated her adult daughter like a baby. She would ask her the same questions as her four-year-old grandchild. *What did you do today? What did you have for dinner?*

A different colleague's wife was the problem, not the colleague himself. She was an accountant. Their son was an accountant. She tried to force him to work with her. He wanted nothing to do with her. His father was no help. Finally, he said he was going to move to Israel and work for ex-pats and Israeli businesses with US subsidiaries.

One day, at lunch, Lynn witnessed these two geniuses bad mouthing the boss and his wife. Their daughter had announced she would marry an Israeli, twice her age, who was not religious and spoke very little English, except for being able to ask for money! Lynn lost it and told them off. She made it clear to them that, just as the boss's daughter had left to get away from her parents, so too had their children left to get away from them.

Ironically, when the boss found out, he thanked her. He had come around. He realized she had been right all along.

VI

JONATHAN was one of my first friends in Israel. He too was an ex-pat Canadian. He was married to Ronit, an Israeli who had, with his help, taught herself English. She helped me with my Hebrew and I helped her with her English.

Jonathan's parents had visited him while they were dating. They were rude and obnoxious to her. He literally sent them packing. She was so impressed by the way he had stood up to them in her defense that there was no question that she would agree to marry him.

Her parents insisted that he invite his parents to the wedding. Reluctantly, he did, but along with the invitation he made it clear to them that if they interfered, criticized or complained about anything, they would never meet their grandchildren. They behaved.

Fast forward a couple of years and Ronit was pregnant. The child was a boy. Despite promises that were made, they did not name him Bruce. (You just can't trust some people!)

I forget the reason, it was not serious, but the *bris* had to be postponed a couple of days. This meant that Jonathan's parents had time to arrive for the ritual circumcision.

Jonathan was worried sick, literally, about how his parents would behave. He was convinced that they would be up to their old tricks. He would have none of it, but he did not want to aggravate or upset his wife. She had had a C-section and was not in the best of moods.

He picked his parents up at the airport. He brought them to his car, opening the front passenger door for his father and the back passenger door for his mother. He told her to wait before she got into the car.

He loaded their bags in the trunk and on the driver's side of the passenger seat. Then he moved to the passenger side. His mother had not waited to get into the car but had sat on an angle between the child's car seat, which Jonathan was about to remove, and the door.

He asked her what she was doing. She said that she did not want to be a nuisance and that sitting that way would be fine.

He physically removed her from the car, along with the bags. He then let it rip.

He reminded her of how she had treated him as a child. He told her she was "a despicable person and human trash." (I'll never forget that!) He said that under no circumstances would he tolerate any more of her "crap." She would not be allowed anywhere near his wife or son. He then returned their bags and the gifts they brought to the terminal entrance. They followed him.

He asked his father if he wanted to meet his grandson. He said he did. He asked him which bag was his. Jonathan picked up the bag and took it and his father back to the car. His mother asked what she should do. He told her...

Jonathan told me that he and his father did not say a word the entire drive from Tel-Aviv to Jerusalem. When they got to the hotel, he told his father that he would come by the following morning at 8:00 to pick him up and take him to his apartment to meet the baby and see his wife.

Just so you understand, his mother knew the hotel where they would be staying and had money for a taxi. She arrived at the hotel an hour or so after her husband. (As he explained it to me, on a certain level his father knew he was right and he hoped that leaving her at the airport would set her straight.)

The next morning Jonathan's father was waiting for him. He started to say something about his mother and Jonathan simply responded, "Do you want to meet your grandson or not?"

When they got to his apartment, Jonathan's mother-in-law stepped in. She told him that it was not right to exclude his mother from the *bris*. For what is called *shlom bayit* – a peaceful home – he relented on one condition: His mother would have to remain by the door (the *bris* was to be in his apartment), would not be permitted to speak, and would not be permitted to touch the baby although he would be shown to her. (That was my job as well as to stand by her and make certain she followed the rules. Sadly, she did. I would have loved to have thrown her out!)

Jonathan's parents cut their visit short and returned home the next day. His mother had learned her lesson. Jonathan took them to the airport (he wanted to make certain they were really leaving!) and told them (really his mother) that since they had followed the rules, he would invite them to the boy's first birthday party. He did. They came. His mother criticized Ronit. Jonathan threw her out and, to the best of my knowledge, never saw her again. His father would visit every few years, by himself, to meet his grandchildren – none of whom were named Bruce, although I swear, their daughter's first word was my name!

VII

ONE of the most disgusting examples I have of Americans moving to Israel is not of Americans moving to Israel, but *being moved* to Israel.

I have always been disgusted by the parents of small children who could not stand up to their own parents and, instead, moved to Israel to get away from them. Luckily, in the few cases in which I was aware, the children were so miserable in Israel that the parents did the right thing and returned home. In some cases sanity ruled when parents saw with whom their children were associating and realized that that was not the environment they wanted for their children.

You see, Israel is not really a "Jewish" state. "Jewish" implies a value. The fact that the majority of Israelis have Jewish maternal grandmothers (the legal definition of a Jew) is meaningless. Almost all Israelis – Jewish, Christian, Druze, or Muslim – have brown hair and brown eyes. Saying Israel is a "Jewish" state is as meaningful as saying it is a "brown-haired brown-eyed" state. Both are equally meaningless and, to be truthful, the latter is more encompassing!

Israel is one of the most divided societies in the world; maybe the most. The Orthodox hate the secular; the secular hate the Orthodox. Conservatives hate liberals; liberals hate conservatives. Ashkenazi Jews hate Sephardi Jews; Sephardi Jews hate Ashkenazi Jews. In fact they have racial slurs for each other!

Orthodoxy is the recognized stream of Judaism. Reform and Conservative clergy are not permitted to officiate at marriages. Non-orthodox Jews are second-class citizens. Israel expects reform and conservative rabbis to preach from their pulpits in Canada and the States in support of Israel, but won't recognize their authority. Not very "Jewish" is it?

And don't laugh. In a strange way Israel itself may have confirmed my opinion. If a law has to be passed which confirms the obvious, maybe the obvious is not so obvious after all. I am, of course, referring to the recently passed Jewish Nation-State Law which, in essence, formalizes Israel as *the* Jewish state. If Israel is really a "Jewish" state, why pass the law?

But I digress.

As bad as bringing young children to Israel is because you are not mature enough to stand up to your parents, bringing elderly parents to Israel is even worse. Children are resilient. They should not have to be, but if they are so inclined, they will usually find a way to survive. Elderly parents, not so much.

I know there appears to be a contradiction here. Up until now I have been talking about getting revenge on "trash." But the "trash" can fight back. It's a fair fight. The children get their parents' money and don't have to deal with them on a daily basis. The parents get to play the "martyr" – *My son lives in a settlement on the West Bank. My daughter is married to an Israeli who can't support her and their children.*

But elderly parents can't defend themselves.

I worked for close to five years at nursing homes, which I why this is a sensitive subject for me. So when I got the call to try and stop adult children, who lived in Israel, from moving their parents to a nursing home in Israel, I knew that this was revenge that crossed the line.

When my friend called to tell me what was happening I asked him to put me in touch with the parents' lawyer. She did.

I met with him and explained what was happening. He said he was not surprised. He had been a friend of the family for decades. I explained that based on my nursing home experience, the most important factor in choosing a nursing home, besides the obvious care-related issues, was having visitors. If these people were moved to Israel, in addition to becoming totally dependent on their children – who hated them, they would have no friends visiting them. They would be alone.

He told me that I was not telling him anything he did not already know. This man was intelligent. He had set up a trust that would pay for the nursing home and provide spending money. In other words, by bringing their parents to Israel, the children would cut themselves off from their parents' money.

Or course, they did not know that. And when they found out, they consoled themselves with the hope that their parents would not be long for this world and they would get their inheritance. What they did not know was that their parents had left their estate to charity. When their parents' lawyer informed them, as he had been instructed to do, the parents knew that they had won. Whatever pressure they had placed on their parents to get them to agree to the move disappeared. The move to Israel was cancelled.

VIII

LISA was different. She would sit with us and if someone was dealing with a parent or family issue, she would listen and was always supportive, but she never contributed to the conversation. The fact that she was sitting in the university cafeteria with us, American and Canadian ex-pats, meant that she too hated her parents, but we had no idea why.

Today, decades later, I understand about repressed memories; at the time, however, I did not.

Every year or so Lisa's parents would visit for a couple of weeks. She did not seem to care. Unlike the rest of us, it did not bother her. They came; they went. No harm, no foul.

Then it happened.

On their flight to Israel they shared a row with an Israeli who had recently gotten out of the Army. He was 21. They liked him and wanted to set him up with Lisa.

When her parents arrived, Lisa left a message for them at the airport that she would not be able to pick them up due to car troubles. That was the truth. I know because she called me to come to the garage and pick her up and take her to the hotel. I was happy to do so.

I went into the hotel with her to answer the call of nature. She waited by Reception and I went to the Men's Room. When I returned, I heard a commotion. All hell had broken lose.

She and her parents were supposed to go to dinner. They invited the Israeli to join them. Lisa was livid.

All the suppressed hatred that had been buried for years came to the surface.

When she was 16, her mother had set her up on a date. She did not want to go but she forced her. I could not tell, and never asked, but he either raped her or tried to rape her. She blamed her mother and refused to date again. She also stopped socializing. As had happened with all of us, she became focused on one thing and one thing only, getting to Israel. Schoolwork came first; socialization was an unnecessary distraction.

Now, as the memories returned, she screamed at her mother. When her father tried to intervene, she pushed him and said that he was useless, had not supported her, and was just as much to blame as her mother.

As Security approached, she told her parents never to contact her again. She announced she did not need their money, was going into the Army, and if they every showed up when she had access to a weapon, she'd kill them!

She pushed the Israeli, who was standing right there, totally confused, out of the way, forgot I was her ride, stormed out of the hotel and got on a bus back to her apartment.

The following day she apologized to me. (I had no idea for what!) I asked her how she was feeling. She started to laugh. Turned out she had a letter from the Army waiting for her when you got home informing her that she had been rejected by the service for a medical reason. When I asked her if her parents ever showed up again if her rejection by the Army meant she would not kill them, she smiled and walked away.

IX

SOME of us had child "boyfriends" or "girlfriends." They were the children of friends or employers who "adopted" us. We became part of their extended families. Some were Israeli, most were immigrants. A few were from Canada or the States.

Having a child friend, aged three, four, five or six, was good for everyone. The parents got free babysitting and an adult they could trust with their child. The child got to play grownup and a trusting adult in whom they could confide if they were afraid to go to their parents with what they considered to be a situation which could "get them in trouble." And we had a surrogate family, could be a "big brother" or "big sister," had help learning Hebrew, and a friend who would tell us the truth about our age appropriate girlfriends or boyfriends (as long as they, the child, knew they were our Number One girl or boyfriend!).

Rachel's "boyfriend" was the sweetest four-year-old you would ever want to meet. We all enjoyed it when she would bring him to campus. As he got older, he asked some pretty good questions. He was always fun.

When Rachel's parents would come to visit, she would become withdrawn. Tzvi, her "boyfriend," helped keep her grounded. As she would tell us, there's no better way to calm down than to cuddle with a four-year-old on your lap, reading a bedtime story, and both of you falling asleep.

What's nice about having a child friend is when, all of a sudden, they no longer act like children. Instead of playing grownup, they actually act grownup.

Her parents wanted to try to repair their relationship with her. That was rare but not unprecedented. Most did not have enough brains to realize their children hated them. That in itself said it all.

Rachel's parents were well-off and decided to throw a small party for her and her friends in their suite at their hotel. They told her to invite 10 friends. She invited 11, including Tzvi. She was taking care of him because his mother had been hospitalized and his father was serving in the Reserves.

Rachel had been teaching Tzvi, who was then six or seven, English.

When she introduced him to her parents as her "boyfriend," her mother responded, "When are you going to get a real boyfriend." She quickly put her mother in her place. Her words were sharp but not her tone. She did not want to upset Tzvi.

Not happy being shown up by Rachel, her mother, truly a piece of human filth, resumed her old ways, delivering one backhanded compliment after the other.

At one point, Tzvi more or less understood what her mother was saying. She criticized her dress, basically saying that it made her look fat.

Tzvi would have none of it. All of a sudden this "child," started defending his girlfriend. He told her mother that he thought she, Rachel, looked beautiful and that she should apologize. Mommy dearest chose to laugh at him instead.

In Hebrew, Tzvi turned to Rachel and told her that her mother was mean and that she, Rachel, had told him that if someone was mean the best thing to do was to walk away.

You can't argue with a six-year-old! Rachel told her parents what he had said and recommended that her mother apologize. She refused.

With Tzvi and Rachel holding hands and leading us, we all left – just as the food was arriving. Being hungry university students we knew what our next move had to be. We asked Tzvi where he wanted to eat. I knew what his answer would be. He had once said that first he loved his parents, second Rachel, and third pizza with lots of cheese.

One of our group actually worked at a pizza place. He walked us over. His boss was surprised that such a large group was showing up. It was a small place and we basically took all the available seats. But he was good man and, when he heard what had happened, he went over to Tzvi and asked him to whom he should give the bill. Tzvi said he had something like five lira and would pay himself. Coincidentally, that was the exact amount of the bill.

Just so you understand, this was when Israel was suffering from hyperinflation. Five lira was probably worth one or two cents. So, Tzvi paid and we left the owner a very nice tip!

When she got home, Rachel's parents called. She said that the only way she would see them was if she could bring Tzvi over and if they guaranteed to apologize to them. They refused.

Waiting for her parents when they returned to the States was a Special Delivery letter from Rachel. In it, ripped up by little hands, was the check they had brought her along with a typewritten letter officially informing them that she disclaimed any inheritance. To the best of my knowledge, she never heard from them again.

X

MISHA was a *refusnik*, a Russian Jew who the Soviets had denied permission to emigrate to Israel. We never knew why or how, but he had been released and joined us at the university.

He did not like Israelis. We did not know why. He did not trust his fellow Russians. He really did not like Americans. As far as he was concerned, they were only interested in helping the famous Russian Jews escape, not the everyday people. In fact, he only liked Canadians. For some reasons he trusted us.

Understand, Misha was totally paranoid. He had a right to be. He believed he was being followed. He believed he was being recorded. The first time we visited him at his apartment he told us to wait outside the door. We figured he wanted to clean up.

At the time, we had not noticed that when he unlocked his apartment door, he did not open it with the knob but pushed the door open while running his fingers along the frame. He always left a piece of thread on the door. If it was broken, he knew someone had entered.

The apartment was a mess. I'm being polite. Leave the windows of your apartment open when a tornado is moving over it and your apartment will look better than his.

Now a "mess" is a "mess" unless you know where everything is. He knew where everything was supposed to be. That's was his second "line of defense," so to speak. Someone might have been able to replace the thread, but no one could put everything in his apartment back where it belonged.

It took years for him to open up about his family, and then only in broad strokes. We did not know if he had any siblings, but he did speak fondly of his parents, about whom he was very worried.

One day he asked me to meet with him. He wanted me to explain how "we" could hate our parents. He did not understand it.

This one was going to be tough. He and his parents had shared fear together. That caused a bond. They had sacrificed for him, agreeing to stay in the Soviet Union in exchange for his being allowed to leave. (That was news that he shared with me when he asked to meet.)

This was going to be *really* tough.

Misha hated the Soviet regime and loved his parents. We hated our parents and loved our countries. We did not abandon Canada or the United States. We abandoned our parents.

I told him my story and that of some of our friends. (I had received their permission in advance.)

As I told him what we had gone through, he began to see parallels between what our parents had done to us and what the Soviet regime had done to him. While the cruelty, the acts, were not the same, psychologically there was no difference.

That realization, and Misha's acceptance of it, saved a lot of people. We were able to put things in a new way, which helped convince some individuals, who were hesitating to break off relations with their parents, that it would be the right thing to do.

Think about what you just read. A man who had been terrorized by his government, forced into exile and who had to abandon his parents, leaving them virtual prisoners, that man, drew the parallel and concluded that our hatred of our parents was analogous to his hatred of the Soviet government. Think about it. He came up with it; I didn't.

XI

WHEN I first arrived at the Hebrew University, I was in what was called the "Four-Year Program." The first year was held at the School for Overseas Students. It was the Preparatory Year, designed to have the student learn Hebrew and to get acclimated.

There was another program, the "One-Year Program," which was the university's year-abroad program. For the most part, the courses available during the first year of the Four-Year Program, were the same as those for the One-Year. The level was far below that of the university proper.

When we were graduate students, one of the professors asked a friend and me to be his teaching assistants, basically to grade the papers of his One-Year Program students. The money was OK, so we agreed.

When we handed in the grades he told us to mark the tests again. We had failed roughly half the students! He explained that the purpose of the School for Overseas Students was (a) to foster immigration to Israel and (b) to bring in foreign currency to the university. Except in rare cases, everyone was to pass. We were prudent. We wanted the money. We didn't really care. Everyone passed.

One of the students in the One-Year Program, Joe, was a really nice guy. He was also smart and wanted to know about transferring to the university proper to complete his bachelor's degree.

Since I worked in the School, he came to me. I found out what he would have to do. His Hebrew was excellent so he met the most difficult requirement, a minimal understanding of the language.

I helped him with the paperwork but, before I submitted it, I asked him to meet with me and some friends. He agreed.

We met in the cafeteria of the School of Education. First, they served the best food. Second, none of his fellow students would be there (it was on the other side of campus). Third, we could have a fairly private conversation, as it was a large cafeteria.

There were three or four us present. Each of us in turn told him why we had moved to Israel. Given that he had expressed an intention to immigrate, we knew that he too must have hated his parents. We wanted him to be comfortable telling us his story. This was a big decision and we wanted to make certain he was doing it for the right reasons and in the right way.

It took a lot to shock us, but he did.

I guess we were naïve. We had all grown up in the sixties and seventies. We must have led secluded lives. We had never heard of "open marriages." Of course, we knew about marital infidelity, but husbands and wives who slept around with their spouse's knowledge, consent and permission was new to us!

Apparently, his father had gotten a woman pregnant and he was sure his mother had had an abortion. (He did not know what became of his half-sibling.) He wanted nothing to do with his parents. He had no respect for them. Their lifestyle literally sickened him.

When he was finished telling us his story, you could have heard a pin drop. None of us knew what to say. There was a definite need for humor. I looked at my friends, I looked at him, I saw the not-yet-eaten piece of cake on my plate, handed it to him and said, "You win!"

Everyone laughed and he successfully transferred.

He asked our advice on how to keep the money flowing from his parents. We advised him to tell them that his tuition would be significantly lower than in the States, but with inflation being what it was, he would need foreign currency. He asked them to send him the "savings." They did.

I was surprised, I'm not sure why, when, a couple of years later, he told me he was getting married. His parents, not having a clue about the contempt in which he held them, asked how much the wedding would cost. He quoted them a very high figure, which they readily paid.

He then had a brilliant idea. He had enough money, with what his parents had sent, his job and his bride's, to live on for a few years, so he could afford to sever all ties with his parents.

XII

I liked Lynn. She had a good sense of humor. She was intelligent. But she was torn. She hated her parents but loved her kid sister. She seriously considered moving to Israel, but did not want to abandon her.

When I returned from Israel, I participated in some Jewish community/pro-Israel events. I found them amusing. The participants had no idea what Israel was all about. As the saying goes, they had drunk the Kool-Aid.

I must not have had on my best poker face because at one such event, when a speaker was talking about Israel being a democracy (it is not, members of Parliament, the *Knesset*, represent political parties not the electorate – akin to the old Soviet system – and it is institutionalized minority rule, despite the trappings of democracy, the secret ballot, independent judiciary, a free press – within limits of national security, freedom of assembly, etc.) I smirked. She noticed, smiled and afterwards we had a nice conversation.

Her sister was about to have her *bat mitzvah*. Let me explain:

According to Jewish Law, girls reach maturity at age 12, boys at age 13. Accordingly, the *bat mitzvah* ceremony is held at age 12 for girls, the *bar mitzvah* ceremony at 13 for boys.

The reason is simple: Girls mature faster than boys. In what is called Reform Judaism, which is basically a membership club where Jewish law has been "modernized" into irrelevancy, because of the sick need of liberals for egalitarianism and equality between the genders – biology be damned! – girls in this Movement are forced to wait a year to become recognized as "adults." Of course, this equality nonsense could have been achieved had boys been granted adulthood at age 12, along with the girls. I don't think I need to explain why that did not happen...

In any event, in Orthodoxy, the parents of girls throw a party for their 12-year-old daughters who deliver a speech about the weekly *Torah* reading corresponding with their birthdays. For Reform Jews, it's basically a Sweet Sixteen party held three years early.

Lynn invited me to the party. In fact, she invited me to meet her parents and sister a few weeks before the party was to be held. Sometimes I have a way with the ladies and her sister and I hit it off. I don't remember what I said or did, but whatever it was, resulted in a major crush. Lynn did not mind. Her parents did not mind. There was nothing wrong with it. It basically manifested itself by her holding my hand when we walked to a nearby restaurant and her wanting to sit next to me.

Then the *bat mitzvah* took place. She was surrounded by her friends, having the time of her life, being the center of attraction. As she should have been.

But then something very unfortunate happened. For whatever reason, she was standing beside me when her father took the microphone. He thanked everyone for coming and then, for some inexplicable reason, said, "Becky is standing over there by Bruce. They met a couple of weeks ago. It was love at first sight. She has a huge crush on him."

At that point she turned and buried her face in my leg. I patted her on the back of her head and, in a loud voice said, "The feeling is mutual; I have a huge crush on her too."

Her father responded, "I thought you would be marrying Lynn not Becky."

My response: "It depends on which one signs the pre-nup."

I was not smiling. Becky was crying. Lynn looked fit to kill.

Lynn came over to us and we calmed Becky down. Her mother joined us, which surprised Lynn. This was the first time Lynn had seen her mother oppose her father.

Some of Becky's friends came over and they moved off to the dessert table. I then read her mother the Riot Act.

I explained to her that Becky would remember what her father had done for the rest of her life. She hated him today, and would hate him in four-five years when she would be applying to universities. If she did not want her to wind up in Israel, if she did not want *both* of her daughters in Israel, she had to deal with this right now.

She went to her husband, grabbed his arm, and took him outside. From the foyer we could hear loud talking, although we could not make out any of the actual words.

When they returned, her father took Becky aside. He asked me to join them. (Lynn and her mother were there.) First he apologized to Becky. Then he thanked me for having stood up for her. He said that he knew that what he had done was wrong, he was sorry, and hoped she would forgive him. Begrudgingly, she agreed and accepted the apology.

Lynn whispered to me that she did not believe he was in the least bit sincere. She was right.

Not ten minutes later, standing next to his wife, and within earshot of Becky and Lynn, he complained to a friend that he had to behave otherwise he would be taken to the woodshed for another whipping. He continued, that he was out of apologies so felt it best to keep his mouth shut.

Here's another reason why I am writing this book now. Three months ago I found out that Lynn and Becky, now 19, had moved to Israel.

XIII

RINAT was the most Israeli of the ex-pats. She had Hebraized her name. She had served in the Army, advancing to the rank of lieutenant. She was smart. She was kind. She was nice. She was attractive. And she was married. At least technically.

I knew she hated her parents. I did not know the details; they were none of my business. Her husband was also an ex-pat. I knew he hated his parents. Again, I did not know why. But that was not the question that intrigued me.

Rinat lived in Jerusalem. She owned her apartment. It was a very nice one-bedroom in the Ramat Eshkol neighborhood where I also lived. We met at the bakery when I had made a linguistic *faux pas* and, instead of asking for a "napkin" to wipe my face, I asked for a different type of napkin... (When she explained my error, I turned ten shades of red and the owner, who from then on had my business for life, refused to charge me for my order!)

I thanked her and offered to share with her whatever pastry I had bought. She politely declined (more on that in a moment), explaining that she only bought bread at the bakery for the Sabbath, and invited me to her apartment for a proper lunch. I saw the wedding band on her finger and realized this was going to be a plutonic friendship, if a friendship developed at all. I had no problem with that. (Remember, the beginning of the book? I like "Pluto!")

We had a normal conversation. Then I asked her about her husband. There was nothing really masculine about the furnishings. It looked like a woman's apartment – whatever that means.

She told me he was an architect and that he lived in Eilat. I asked if she rented her apartment for the academic year. That was when she told me she owned it. I then ask if she rented it out when class was out, as another friend did, who rented it to foreign visitors for hard currency. She said that she did not, that she lived there year-round.

Understand the geography. Jerusalem, if traffic is on your side, which it never is, is a four-hour drive to Eilat which is a little more than 200 miles away. It's six-seven hours by bus (because you have to go through Tel-Aviv), which makes it 40-50 miles longer, depending on the route).

This living arrangement was strange. I, a man, as already noted, who swore that he would never marry and never have children in order to achieve the ultimate revenge of killing off his family line, would have seriously considered marrying this woman. She was that impressive. So why the long-distance marriage? It made no sense. Then I met her husband.

One day I was going to be in her neighborhood and called to see if I could drop by. I had moved to a new apartment on the other side of town, but we had stayed in touch. She told me her husband was there. I heard him tell her to invite me for dinner. She did and I accepted.

On my way I stopped at the bakery and bought a pie. When I arrived, Shmuel, her husband, answered the door.

After the normal pleasantries I handed him the pie. He thanked me and, in a low voice, explained that Rinat had a weight problem. She had been obese as a child and young woman – in fact, until she immigrated. He warned me that she would thank me and then decline the gift, putting it in the fridge and asking me to take it with me when I left. That was exactly what happened.

Rinat told us to sit in the living room and get to know each other. We did. I liked him and, according to Rinat, he liked me.

As we were talking, I began to be aware of a few things about him. When he got up and went to the kitchen to bring out some cold drinks, I noticed something else.

Shmuel had many of the physical attributes of a homosexual. His gait was off; his posture was off; he had a lisp. When he was concentrating, he was able to control them all. But when he was relaxed, and felt he was among friends, which he was, he forgot himself and his homosexuality became more evident.

Obesity and homosexuality. I did not have to ask; I knew exactly what had happened. My suspicions were confirmed when I served in the Army.

My Army experience was bad. Suffice it to say that I developed an ulcer, sued and won my law suit against the Army. During my service, one member of the unit I was in, a newcomer, was clearly homosexual. His arrival gave the 18- and 19-year-olds I was serving with (I was 27) a new target. Instead of tormenting me, they tormented him.

One day I ran into Rinat. She asked me how I was doing. I told her the truth and mentioned the homosexual. She then confided in me that Shmuel had had similar experiences when he had served in the Army. For whatever reason, she felt the need to open up and she told me their story:

They had grown up in the same town. They were brought together by bullying and teasing. In order to deflect the charges of homosexuality, Shmuel wanted to get married. For him it was simple. He thought that was the best way to prove his tormentors wrong. She told me that when they finally announced their wedding, he enjoyed pointing out that he was about to be married and they weren't. He was 22; she was 18.

When they arrived, he already had his degree in architecture and a job offer. When she arrived, she began her undergraduate studies at the Hebrew University.

Let's deal with Shmuel first:

When I was in high school, the anti-Semites would call me "kike," "Christ killer," or "fag." That was the closest interaction I had with homosexuality. No doubt some of them were "projecting," but I was focused on my studies and getting accepted to the Hebrew University. Homosexuality was of no interest to me at all and their insults meant nothing. I had no social life of which to speak because I could not risk bringing anyone into my house. In any event, I wanted no distractions from my goal of putting as much distance as possible between myself and my relatives. (Once I got to Israel I began to socialize and take advantage of all the possibilities of youth on which I had missed out. The advantage I had was that at the Hebrew University there were no fraternities. Given that Israeli students were almost all post-military service, they were there to learn not to play. I was use to "seriousness" and, after a year or so, began to flourish.)

I don't remember the circumstances, but when homosexuality came up in a discussion at university, I considered it to be a mental health disorder. Something had to be wrong with these people. Later, when I read Darwin, *On the Origin of Species*, and was interested in homosexuality because some of my career counseling clients had the disorder, I focused on his use of the term "variety" within the context of a subset of a species. To my way of thinking, homosexuals who, by definition, add nothing to the continuance of the species except if they go against their nature, must be a variety of *homo sapiens*.

If you think about it, homosexuality has to be an abnormality. After all, how can a homosexual species exist? If there is no natural tendency to procreate, a species would die.

I remember reading an op-ed by a psychiatrist who confirmed my thoughts. Trouble is, I can't find it so you will have to trust me on this. He wrote that the frontal lobes of a homosexual's brain must be deformed causing improper decision making when dealing with sexual orientation. I know I read it because that was the first time I had become aware of frontal lobes and, when studying decision making, I remembered the term and incorporated a little biology into a paper I wrote.

In any event, years later, in fact last year, I accidentally came across an unimpeachable source for the fact that homosexuality is a mental health disorder. In *The Ego and the Id*, Freud writes about "The study of mild cases of homosexuality..." If homosexuality was not a mental health disorder, Freud would not have written about it and he certainly would not have referred to "mild cases." The only question I needed to ask was, Is homosexuality still considered a mental health disorder?

According to a September 18, 2015 post, written by Dr. Neal Burton on the *Psychology Today* website, in 1968 homosexuality was listed as a mental disorder. Now, given the obvious sensitivity of the topic, and the fact that I call already hear the liberals charging me with homophobia, I quote from the article:

> *In 1973, the American Psychiatric Association (APA) asked all members attending its convention* [Just as an aside, note that they asked all members *attending* the convention, they did not poll their entire membership. It would have been interesting to see the results if they had.] *to vote on whether they believed homosexuality to be a mental disorder. 5,854 psychiatrists voted to remove homosexuality from the DSM* [the Diagnostic and Statistical Manual of Mental Disorders], *and 3,810 to retain it.*
>
> *The APA then compromised, removing homosexuality from the DSM but replacing it, in effect, with "sexual orientation disturbance" for people "in conflict with" their sexual orientation. Not until 1987 did*

> *homosexuality completely fall out of the DSM.*
>
> *Meanwhile, the World Health Organization (WHO) only re-moved homosexuality from its ICD* [International Classification of Diseases] *classification with the publication of ICD-10 in 1992, although ICD-10 still carries the construct of "ego-dystonic sexual orientation". In this condition, the person is not in doubt about his or her sexual preference, but "wishes it were different because of associated psychological and behavioral disorders".*

What makes this so sad, decades after the events related herein, is that it is now clear that the "help," if any, homosexuals are given is not really "help" at all. Among end-stage homosexuals, persons who undergo "sex change" operations, the suicide rate is significantly higher than that of the general population (https://www.ncbi. nlm.nih.gov/pmc/ articles/PMC5436370/). It may make liberals feel better that they have created an atmosphere in which homosexuals can have their bodies mutilated, but it does nothing for those suffering from the disorder (https://www.heritage.org/gender/commentary/sex-reassignment-doesnt-work-here-the-evidence).

Bottom line, Shumel was a homosexual who could function in society. He did not walk around wearing women's clothing and acting effeminate. He knew the difference between right and wrong, acceptable and unacceptable behavior. He could and did work in a professional setting and was respected by his peers. But, apparently, not by his parents.

In the days when homosexuality was clearly seen as a mental disorder, which is why I included my previous statements on the subject, Shumel had gone to his parents seeking help. He knew he was sick. His parents demurred. They forbade him from talking about it to anyone, including his pediatrician. They told him to "man up" and ridiculed him any time he did something "wrong," from the way he carried a bag (not by the hand but the arm "like women do") to his posture.

When he overheard his parents say that they would have to "beat the fag out of him," he did not know if they were being literal or figurative. He knew he needed out and confided in his young friend, Rinat.

Crying, he told her what he had overheard. She totally empathized and told him that she planned to move to Israel to get away from her parents, especially her mother, who would humiliate her because of her weight. Her mother tried to shame her into being thin!

The final straw for her was her *bat mitzvah.* By all accounts, she had done a great job. She gave a talk that was truly inspirational. Everyone sincerely complimented her on it. In fact, someone from the local newspaper who had been invited wanted to publish it! She had done very well.

While everyone was congratulating her, she overheard her mother say, "She's such a smart girl. Why can't she lose weight? Why does she have to be my 'fat so'?" That did it. Just as I had done after my *bar mitzvah*, she started focusing on Israel and Israeli universities as her salvation.

When they realized how much they shared, Shmuel and Rinat planned their escape. Shmuel had an Israeli friend who introduced him to an Israeli architect. He flew to Israel and, as noted, got a job with a firm. It was to work on a project in Eilat. At the same time, Rinat was accepted to the Hebrew University.

They both planned to immediately break off all ties with their parents, but they wanted to get as much money out of them as possible. And, as she admitted, their relatives were no prizes either. None had supported her. None had offered comfort. And they all knew what she was going through. Shmuel's relatives were no better.

Immediately after Rinat graduated high school, they announced that they were going to be married and that it would be a small affair. Their parents, on the other hand, invited a few of their (the parents') friends and relatives, but also many business associates, making the reception into a business occasion. Given that they were moving to Israel the day after the reception, they let it be known that they did not want any presents but would appreciate money.

Their plan worked. Their parents agreed to give them a nice sum which they had asked for given how much they had saved their parents by having a small reception and letting their parents organize it so they (apparently) could claim a tax write-off (!). The guests all chipped in with checks.

Now came time for revenge. Immediately after the Reception Line concluded, the gifts duly handed over in nice white envelopes, they said good-bye to their parents and left. When the rabbi stopped them at the door and asked where they were going, they let him know that they were leaving, why they were leaving, and made it quite clear that they would never have anything to do with their parents again.

Rinat told me that she heard that after they left, the reception continued like nothing had happened, despite the fact that the rabbi had reported to their parents what he had been told. The friends and relatives didn't care and the business guests were too confused, and polite, to ask any questions.

They never heard from their parents again. (By the way, all the checks were deposited in an Israeli bank and they all cleared!)

XIV

MICHAEL hated his younger brother Larry. The difference in their ages was only 19 months. Until Michael turned 17, relations between the brothers were excellent.

When the brothers were young, they both had a crush on their babysitter. At that point their parents, rightly, established a simple rule: No fighting over girls. Whoever meets her first, gets first right of rejection.

A good rule. On Michael's 17th birthday, he introduced the family to his 16-year-old girlfriend. Larry liked her and asked her out. He broke the rule! She accepted his invitation and Michael dumped her. He blamed Larry, not the girl. Right or wrong, that destroyed the relationship.

But it was the response of his parents that bothered Michael the most. Instead of chastising Larry, they supported him. They liked the girl and had no problem when Larry would invite her to family events. For Michael, that was rubbing salt in an open wound.

Whatever the event, including attending religious services, he would refuse to attend if "she" was going to be there.

Michael stopped speaking with Larry. He ignored him. He would have nothing to do with him. One evening, while the brothers were eating dinner with their parents, Larry started to choke. Michael was certified in CPR and knew how to perform the Heimlich maneuver. His parents begged him to save Larry. He refused until they promised never to have "her" at any family event and to pay him what it would have cost them if he had attended the local college. He knew the amount, told them, and explained he wanted the money to move Israel. They agreed and he saved his brother.

Of course, legally and morally the agreement was not binding. If there is a better example of "duress," I don't know what it is and doubt anyone could come up with one. But by then Michael had done his research. He had been accepted to the University of Haifa (I met him when he came to Jerusalem for a symposium) and knew that he would have plenty of money left over after he paid his tuition and incidental costs. He rightly estimated that, even without working, he'd have enough money for four years.

More importantly, both of his parents had friends with children in Israel. He had reached out to them asking why they had moved to Israel. Their answers were unconvincing. They spoke in terms of Zionist ideals. He did not believe them for a minute.

He told his parents, when they objected to giving him the money, that he would tell everyone that he was moving to Israel because of how they had hurt him, just like their friends had done to their kids, who were now living in Israel. (He did not know that to be a fact, at least not yet. It was a guess and a bluff.) He made it clear that they could keep their money and lose their friends, or give him the money and keep their friends. In either case, once he graduated high school, he would be gone.

The bluff worked. They paid. And when he got to Israel, and met his correspondents, they confirmed that he had guessed correctly. Of course, he did not know why they hated their parents, but hate them they did.

XV

PRIOR to his *bar mitzvah*, Richard had been teased by his parents. While he knew the *Torah* reading and how to conduct services, and had written a great speech – everything he was expected to do on his *bar mitzvah* – he suffered from serious stage fright. For him it was truly a phobia.

Years ago a survey was taken asking respondents of what they were most afraid. Public speaking beat out dying for first place. This caused Jerry Seinfeld to opine, "Given the choice between being in the box or delivering the eulogy, most people would choose the box!"

Richard told me that he had actually considered the box as an alternative to his *bar mitzvah*. Luckily, he had a good relationship with his pediatrician and confided in him. (Perhaps if Shmuel, about whom I wrote previously, had had a similar relationship with his pediatrician, his life might have been very different.)

The good doctor helped him. I don't know if it was medication, counseling or both, but the result was not what the doctor had expected. Instead of having the courage to perform his *bar mitzvah* duties, he had the courage to tell his parents to go to hell. He told them off in no uncertain terms. He told them exactly how he felt hearing their ridicule. He made it perfectly clear that he would not attend his *bar mitzvah* and when asked by anyone what was happening, he would tell them the truth.

They did not believe him. The Saturday after he had read them the Riot Act, he went to Services. The rabbi, from the pulpit, mentioned that Richard would be having his *bar mitzvah* in a few weeks. Richard responded.

Seated because his legs were shaking so violently he could not stand, he told the rabbi that he was wrong. He told him, and the entire congregation, that he would not conduct services. And he told everyone exactly why.

His parents were humiliated. But Richard was smart. That Monday he went to school and spoke to a counselor. He told her what he had done and that he was afraid of his parents. He wanted to be put in what he called, "protective custody."

This was unprecedented and no one knew what to do. The counselor called the rabbi and the rabbi called his parents. They were mortified. As bad as things were, if Richard convinced the authorities to remove him from their home, they might lose their other children as well.

An agreement was reached: He would remain in his parents' home. They would pay all of his expenses including the price of his ticket to Israel and his undergraduate studies, as well as cover his incidental costs, including housing and books. And he agreed to have his *bar mitzvah,* but no speech, no conducting of services, and no party. All he would do was to recite the prayer over the *Torah*, known as an *aliyah*, which is a privilege reserved for men who have reached the age of maturity.

Richard never had a real conversation again with his parents. Their mutual hatred was palpable. The rabbi acted as intermediary whenever there was a problem and, as part of the agreement, visited every day and hosted him on the Sabbath and holidays. His daughter lived in Israel and he did not want it known that her relationship with him and his wife was only slightly better than Richard's was with his parents.

The only relative with whom Richard would ever have anything like a real relationship was his invalid grandmother who lived in a nursing home. A few years after he moved to Israel, Richard heard that she had passed away. He sat *shiva* for her. When, a year later, he heard that his mother had died, he threw a party.

XVI

YOUR tenth birthday is special. You have reached double digits! Now you are a big boy or a big girl. It's a good feeling. Unless, of course, your parents are garbage.

Karen had a hard and fast rule: no birthday parties. Period! She had a boyfriend who didn't believe her. He had asked her what she wanted for her birthday. She said, "Absolutely nothing. I don't celebrate it. No presents. Not even a card." Period! End of sentence. End of discussion.

Well her boyfriend didn't get it. He invited a number of us to his father's restaurant. To keep the secret a secret, he did not tell any of us what he was planning. If he had, those who knew would have advised against it. Karen and I were not that close and I did not know about her disdain for birthdays, but it was not uncommon.

In any event, we were in the back room reserved for private parties. His parents had gone all out. The room was nicely decorated and the food was probably excellent. It looked great.

When Karen arrived the hostess directed her to the back room. As she approached, her boyfriend's father welcomed her and opened the door slightly. She pushed it open and we all yelled "Surprise!"

And boy were we ever!

Her boyfriend said "Happy Birth…" He never got to "day." She hauled off and broke his nose with her right hand and his jaw with her left. Karen had served in the Army and was a self-defense expert.

I honestly don't remember who took him to the hospital. I don't think an ambulance was called.

We got her out of the restaurant and took her to her apartment. My car was parked closest to the restaurant so she, and two of her friends, piled into it. For the 10-15 minutes it took to arrive at our destination I heard a string of profanities in English, Hebrew and Arabic, most of which were new to me. She was shaking so violently from anger that my car was vibrating. She was inconsolable.

Her two friends were Israelis. They did not have a clue. They looked at me. We had met maybe half an hour earlier. I told them that I had a feeling what had happened.

On many occasions I had explained to Israelis that Americans and Canadians immigrate to Israel to get away from their parents. At first I was honest and clearly mentioned "hatred," but, as I indicated earlier, I quickly learned that that was not a wise step. They found it hard to believe and were personally insulted. They would be offended and would stop listening. So I would say, "To get away from family/parents/relatives."

I told the two women that my guess was that she had had a bad birthday experience and that that was the catalyst to her decision to immigrate to Israel. "She probably wanted to get away from her parents." I added that, whatever had happened, probably happened when she was very young, at or around her birthday, and the surprise party brought back bad memories. I also guessed that she had expressly told her boyfriend that she does not celebrate her birthday. Having the surprise party brought back bad memories and she responded to what amounted to a psychological attack.

Ironically, a similar occurrence had happened to me, sort of. I was dating a lovely Israeli. Her father was an attorney. We had met in the Law Library at the university. I was reading a book in Hebrew and did not understand something. He saw me using a Hebrew-English dictionary and offered to help. After a while, his daughter showed up and nature began to take its course.

As I mentioned earlier, it was always my intent never to marry so I would kill off my family line. Suffice it to say, sometimes I reconsidered. This was one of those times.

We hit it off. I liked her and her brother. Of course, I had a good relationship with her father. In the beginning, everything was fine with her mother. Then one day she asked me about my family. I told her I had nothing to do with any of them. She asked me why. I told her it was a subject I did not discuss. Her husband stepped in and ended the conversation.

I have never been able to understand why anyone in their right mind would offer a woman jewelry in exchange for their agreeing to marry them. I have never been able to understand why anyone in their right mind would accept a piece of jewelry in exchange for their agreeing to marry someone. While legally it is not a bribe, morally it is. Why is it not considered an insult? After all, the woman does not own the ring until she fulfils her side of the bargain. And if she doesn't, and is so requested, she has to return it.

My thinking is that if you have achieved something in your life worth protecting, and you believe your future is worth protecting, you get engaged by signing a pre-nuptial agreement. And if you have achieved nothing in your life worth protecting, and don't believe your future is worth protecting, why would anyone want to marry you?

So when things got serious, we discussed the pre-nup. At the time, they were not popular in Israel but I made it clear I would not get married without one. I insisted on a marriage of equals and either a divorce of equals or a death of equals and that meant a pre-nup.

Her father was ecstatic. Her mother did not care. She was only interested in the reception, something I made clear I had no interest in and did not want to hear about. I promised to attend, and that was it.

One evening at her parent's home for dinner, her mother asked me, "What would you do if I were to invite your family to the wedding?" Without missing a beat, I replied, "I'd kill you." And I said it in the same tone of voice and with the same emotion as I might have said, "I am wearing black trousers," if she had asked what I was wearing.

Ironically, at the time, I had been working on a paper on the legal issues surrounding self-defense. Mother was in shock. Girlfriend was in shock. Father was curious.

I told him that, in my opinion, a psychological attack – which inviting my family would have been – was no different than a physical attack. Both cause harm. If the one gives the victim the right to defend themselves, so does the other.

I don't remember what else I said, this was a long time ago, but I must have gotten my point across because, when I finished, he said to his wife, "He may be right and I would defend him."

That ended the conversation.

The next time I went out with my girlfriend I insisted, just to be on the safe side, that the wedding be very small. She only had a handful of first-degree relatives and friends, I only had a handful of friends, and with her parents friends (after all, they were paying for it so I recognized that they had the right to invite close friends), I put the limit at 50 people, including the rabbi.

So when Karen went nuts, responding violently to an "attack," I empathized. Even though her Hebrew was fluent (she spoke what was usually referred to as "a beautiful Hebrew"), when she calmed down she spoke in English. Her two girlfriends both spoke English, so it was not a problem. They must have assumed that she was speaking English for my benefit, although I believed it was just easier for her given her agitated state.

When she regained her composure she asked me why I had moved to Israel. "I hate my parents and have no use for any of my relatives." "Good," was her response. And then she told the three of us her story:

Karen's mother was involved with different Jewish women's organizations. They would raise money for this or that cause. But sometimes it felt like all they really did was gossip. And their favorite pastime was matchmaking. It was amazing to hear, but her mother actually tried to set her up when she was 10! That was something of which I had never heard.

She was not interested in dating. She was interested in whatever 10-year-old girls were interested in. In her case, it was not boys! And she certainly did not appreciate being set up. She made it clear to her mother that she was not interested. She incorrectly thought that that was the end of it.

One day, when she came home from school, a very nice and innocent 10-year-old boy and his aunt were waiting at the dinner table to meet her. The aunt was a friend of her mother's and the boy had just moved to the city.

Karen was polite and she was tired. She had just come from an afterschool activity and wanted to change. So she excused herself, went upstairs, took a bath, changed her clothes, and started to do her homework, like she did every day when she returned home from school.

Her mother went to her room and complained that she was being rude. She said that she had told her friend all about her and they thought that she and the boy would make "a cute couple." Even at nine years' of age, Karen had a temper. She let her mother have it with both barrels. She told her that she had said she was not interested in being set up. She did not want a boyfriend. She thought the entire thing was "creepy." She said her mother should mind her own business.

The downstairs guests heard everything. Karen's mother apologized to them (not to her!). When Karen's father came home, and heard what had happened, he sided with his wife. In and of itself, that was not the mistake. The mistake was Karen's punishment: they cancelled her upcoming tenth birthday party.

Karen was lucky. She had friends. One of them was a 15-year-old whose brother was moving to

Israel. The friend knew his reasons. They were close. He also knew Karen's story. Karen asked if the three of them could meet. (Remember, this was a 9-year-old girl, about to turn 10!)

The brother explained to Karen that he was going to apply to a university in Israel. He said he was focused on his studies and had stopped all non-Jewish related extra-curricular activities. He had been told that grades and SAT scores were the most important criteria for acceptance to an Israeli university, but some Jewish-related extracurricular activities could be helpful.

Karen adopted his strategy. She became very cold to her parents. She always behaved. She did well in school. The only time she became belligerent was if they wanted to throw a birthday party for her or if they wanted her to accompany them on a vacation. She made it clear that if they forced her to go with them, she would scream and holler the entire time. They believed her; she stayed with friends.

When she was finally accepted to the Hebrew University, they asked her for permission to throw a going-away party for her. She figured she would get cash gifts, so she agreed. And she was right. Her parents even gave her a nice check.

She deposited all the checks in her bank account and, once they cleared, bought Travelers' Checks. At the airport (she smiled when she got to this part of the story) she reminded her parents what they had done to her on her tenth birthday. She said she told them, "You can both drop dead and go to hell. As far as I am concerned, as of this moment you are both dead!"

As she was flying to Israel, even though this was before the TSA and current airport security, she realized she was standing near Israeli security and was smart enough not to lose her temper. She told me that she had remained calm and even had a smile on her face. She said she doubted anyone heard because she had told her parents that she wanted a little privacy to say good-bye so they stepped over to the side far enough away for the line of passengers and the security personnel who were interviewing them.

She enjoyed remembering and that fully relaxed her.

Needless to say, her relationship with her boyfriend came to a violent end. There were no legal ramifications for the beating. Her boyfriend was an Israeli and he did not want the embarrassment of bringing charges against a woman a good foot shorter than he was, and at least 30 pounds lighter, for assault. His macho Israeli pride and ego saved her. Plus there was the little matter of him having disregarded her wishes, something most people would have classified as disrespectful, although I doubt many who have felt that justified her reaction.

AFTERWORD

ONE day when I arrived at work a colleague did not realize I was standing by the door. I had stopped to tie my shoe, not to eavesdrop. Suddenly I heard a new hire ask her, "What's Bruce like?" Before I had a chance to cough or otherwise let my presence be known, I heard her say, "He's the best friend and worst enemy anyone can have."

On hearing that, smile on my face, I turned around, waited for a minute, and then entered the office not giving any indication that I had overheard her compliment. She had made my day, week, month and year. I could not have been more pleased. What greater compliment than for someone to say that you take care of your friends...and your enemies? And the fact that she had no idea I was standing by the door made it a sincere compliment.

I like revenge. There is something poetic about it – revenge, that is, which is done right. I would go so far as to say it is "beautiful." As I once told to a friend, "I don't know what it is like to have a doctor hand you your baby and tell you that she is perfect, but I do know what it is like to know that you have destroyed an enemy. Except for being told your baby is healthy, I can't imagine a better feeling."

But it has to be done right.

There are six components to, let's call it, "thoughtful revenge."

First, wait. As the saying goes, "Revenge is a dish best served cold." That apparently comes from Eugène Sue's novel, *Memoirs of Matilda*, which was translated into English by D. G. Osbourne and published in 1846. So credit must be given to the French (although, as *Star Trek* fans know, it also comes from Klingon who, personally, I'd rather give it to!).

Its meaning is clear: Wait, don't react! It's good advice. You should never act or react in anger. Take a deep breath. Compose yourself. If not, you'll make a mistake. You'll make matters worse. So calm yourself. Personally, I once waited over a decade to get my revenge. (Actually, to be perfectly honest, I did that twice.)

The second saying that comes to mind and which is important if you don't heed the previous bit of advice, is credited to Confucius, perhaps erroneously, but who cares? "Before you embark on a journey of revenge, dig two graves." That meaning is also clear: Yes, you may kill your enemy, but you may also die yourself. Thus the serving the "dish cold" advice!

Second, have the right motivation. Seek revenge to clear your name or for a societal good, by which I mean to teach your enemy that they cannot get away with such behavior without paying a price.

Third, come up with a plan. Think it through. Keep it simple. Plans, by their very nature, change as circumstances change. Someone once said, "No plan survives first contact with the enemy." That's true in a military campaign, getting revenge and, for that matter, anything else. The more parts to a plan, the more things that can go wrong, so keep it simple. And remember, you cannot control the reactions of others. You have to be ready to improvise.

Fourth, don't seek credit. Yes, you want your enemy to know that you were the one who hurt them. But, except if you are clearing your name, letting them know that you were the one who succeeded in taking them down will only result in a never-ending cycle of revenge. That is no way to live. But there is a problem with this:

Let's say a colleague costs you your job. You get your revenge. If they don't know it was you, then they won't learn that they can't do to others what they did to you. It's a moral dilemma to which I have no solution.

Fifth, keep it legal. You never want to lower yourself to your enemy's level – or beneath that level. What's the point in getting revenge if you wind up in jail? For that matter, what's the point in getting revenge if you wind up in civil court? Which is why you never claim credit.

And finally, sixth, don't hurt innocents.

If you can't achieve all seven, at least bide your time, keep it legal and have a plan for success. You don't want your enemy to beat you twice.

For the record, I never considered my immigration to Israel as revenge. I always thought of it as a journey to freedom and sanity. I was not interested in revenge; I was interested in having a normal life. I wanted to escape. I could have stayed in Canada and still killed off my parents' line. I only learned from my fellow ex-pats that revenge was part of *their* calculus. They were interested in money; I wasn't. I had saved enough to pay my own way and worked almost from the day of my arrival.

That is why this book is not about revenge. It is about bad parenting. But my concern is that people will use it as a blueprint for revenge. Thus this final chapter.

Let me give you a couple of examples of revenge done right. Hopefully, in this way, I can end this book in such a manner that will leave a smile on the reader's face and give them some food for thought. Neither of these examples has anything to do with Israel.

*****

George was thrilled. He finally had saved enough money to purchase his first home. He was single and worked long hours. For him, his house was a refuge from the noisy neighbors who had surrounded him in his apartment. Or so he had hoped.

When he arrived, some of the neighbors welcomed him. About two weeks after he moved in, one neighbor came by with a complaint. The neighbor was upset with the way George was maintaining his property. While he mowed the lawn and trimmed the bushes, unlike all the other houses on the block, he did not have the work done by a professional landscaper. The neighbor, who lived directly across the street, complained that George was lowering his property values.

George literally laughed in his face, told him he was trespassing and warned him that then next time he caught him on his property he would call the Police.

A few days later George received a registered letter from his neighbor informing him that if he did not properly maintain his property he would report him to the municipality.

George ignored the threat. Then he found out that the neighbor actually had gone to a city council meeting and complained about him, by name. Someone had recorded the session, which was broadcast on the local cable access channel.

The response of the mayor and the council members was to politely brush him off. When George went to City Hall to see what he could do, he was told that his neighbor was a known "troublemaker," that he, George, was not doing anything wrong, and to just forget about him.

George didn't. He wanted revenge.

But he was emotional. So he called a friend for advice. The friend said he would come over in a couple of days. This gave George time to calm down.

In the meantime, the neighbor sent another letter to George warning him that if he did not fix up his property by the Fourth of July weekend, when there would be a block party hosted by one of his, George's, neighbors, he would take legal action against him.

When George's friend arrived, he assumed George would have calmed down. He did not know about the new letter. His was the calmer head and, luckily, the calmer head prevailed.

The friend read the letter and told George, "Do what he asks."

Well George was not happy. And he did not understand why his friend was smiling.

The neighbor had demanded three things: that George hire a professional landscaper; that the work be completed before the holiday weekend; and that George not use a chemical fertilizer. And that was the key.

The friend told George that the neighbor had provided all the information necessary for effective revenge, the goal being to get the neighbor to leave him alone. To do that, he needed to make certain that the neighbor lost all support. You see, George had discovered that while no one liked the neighbor, no one wanted to confront him, so they simply gave in to his demands. The man was a bully.

So what did George know? One of his neighbor's, in an adjacent house, was going to host a Fourth of July party, which probably meant an outside barbeque. If George ruined the party, following the neighbor's demands, the neighbor would be blamed, not George.

And that is exactly what happened.

The plan was simple. George's friend told him to reread the letter. He did. And he was still agitated. So he had him read the letter again. He got madder. Then, as he was reading the letter for the final time, George's friend slapped him on the shoulder when he got to "fertilizer." Then George smiled.

The landscaper showed up on Thursday and did the work. The neighbor was ecstatic. He actually went to all the other neighbors' homes and took credit for "saving their property values."

Then Friday morning came. After the neighbor had gone to work, the landscaper returned. Per the letter, George had not permitted the landscaper to use chemical fertilizer. Friday morning the most natural of natural fertilizers arrived.

When the landscaper started to dump the manure, the neighbor's – the wives – all came out to complain. The smell. The mosquitoes. What about the party?

George simply showed them the letter. The wives called their husbands. The husbands called the neighbor who left work and returned home.

The minute he stepped foot on George's property, with the landscaper and his crew as witnesses, George ordered him to leave. He refused. George called the Police and pressed charges against him for trespassing.

If the neighbor had been smart, he simply would have left. George would have signed the complaint and the process would have taken its course. But George had humiliated the man in front of his neighbors. George was now in charge. So when the Police told him, the neighbor, to go home, he resisted. It's one thing to yell profanities at your neighbor, it's a totally other matter to push and shove a police officer.

George waited. George had a plan. George did not break any laws. George's motivation was honorable – to get his crazy neighbor to leave him alone. No innocent person was hurt. (The neighbors were happy to be rid of His Majesty and did not care that the party was cancelled.) Of course, the neighbor had to know that it was George who was acting against him, but five out of six ain't bad!

Just to end the story: All of the neighbors blamed their deposed king for what had happened. They stopped paying attention to him. Within three months, he moved.

*****

Sally was a threat to her boss. She was the person who cleaned up his messes. She was the person who deserved the credit for his successes.

And he wanted her gone. So he set her up and got her fired. Sally wanted revenge.

But she was smart. The company was small and growing. Why get revenge against a midget when, if you are patient and wait a few years, you might be able to take down a giant.

Sally was fired because of inappropriate behavior. Foolishly, she had accepted an invitation to go out with the boss's son who, being of the same moral caliber as his father, claimed she had offered to have sex with him if he helped her to get his father off her back. (He also worked at the company.)

It was "he said-she said," and she lost.

So Sally wanted revenge against father and son.

Junior started working at the company after having completed his bachelor's degree in Social Work, probably the easiest subject in any accredited college, short of "Gender Studies" which, as one comedian noted, "was majoring in unemployment!" And intellectual, he was not. He was a joke. No one took him seriously. He was tolerated, nothing more.

Sally had been right, and a few years after her dismissal she found out, from employees in the company with whom she had kept in touch, that there was a good chance the company was going to be bought out. They told her that father and son were already figuring out how to spend the money!

Now was the time to act.

The father was totally devoted to his son. He worshipped the grown he crawled on! If anything was wrong with the son, if he had any problem, he would obsess over it and would not be able to concentrate. That's was Sally's plan. She would cause the son a problem, by so doing compromise the father, and ruin the sale because the father would not be able to make any decisions.

The plan was simple. She set Junior up with a friend, Nancy, who was more than happy to assist. Of course, Junior had no idea that the new love of his life was a close friend of Sally's.

The two dated. The romance blossomed. Things moved along very quickly. Nancy refused to sleep with Junior. She made it clear that she would not be intimate with him unless they were engaged. (She explained to Junior, and this was true, that her previous boyfriend had proposed to her but had been killed in a freak accident before they were married.) So he proposed and she accepted.

Sadly, for Junior, Nancy got "sick" right after eating the dinner he had prepared in his apartment, where he had proposed and she had accepted. There would be no romance that evening.

Nancy went home. The next morning she called Junior to say that she was going to the doctor and would call him that evening. She did neither.

The first thing the following morning, at work, Junior received a package. It contained the engagement ring and a note, from Nancy, explaining that she had obviously been ill when she agreed to marry him, was returning the ring, and wished him well.

Both the boss and Junior, for whatever reason, insisted that their secretaries open their mail. So everyone in the company knew what had happened to Junior. They could barely hide their glee. Whenever father or son entered a room, everyone stopped talking. Few people could look at Junior with a straight face. Junior was humiliated and his father was distraught, so distraught, in fact, that the sale of the business fell through.

Sally was concerned that if she was successful, and the sale collapsed, that her friends at the company would be hurt. That was not the case. The buyers had done their homework. They were more interested in the staff than in the actual company. So all of Sally's friends applied to the former buyer for jobs and they were all hired. That was also part of the plan. Not only did she want to ruin the sale, she wanted to ruin the company by costing it their best employees. She advised them, and they took her advice, to make a point of being very cooperative with the buyer and their representatives as they were conducting their due diligence prior to the purchase.

*****

Now, to bring this book full-circle, the most important criteria in raising your children is to show them respect and to teach them dignity. Remember that! It might save you from being the subject of a future book...

ABOUT THE AUTHOR

AS a child growing up Bruce Hurwitz was a committed Zionist. He volunteered for, and supported, Israel Bonds and the Canadian Friends of the Hebrew University.

In 1977, in an effort to literally put the maximum amount of distance between himself and his relatives, he moved to Israel for his undergraduate studies at the Hebrew University of Jerusalem. After completing his graduate studies, with honors, he enlisted in the Army, where he served for a year and half. On the day that he was honorably discharged, he sued the Army for the ulcer which had been caused by the maliciousness to which he had been subjected by his fellow soldiers and officers. He won his suit.

After he concluded his doctoral studies at Hebrew University, he returned to Canada where he had lived prior to immigrating to Israel and, after a year, moved to the United States, where he had been born. He worked as a fundraiser and non-profit professional for Jewish and non-Jewish organizations, eventually becoming an executive recruiter.

For the past nine years, as president of Hurwitz Strategic Staffing, he has offered staffing and career counseling services to a plethora of for-profit and non-profit corporations and individuals. The mission of his company is to promote the hiring of veterans.

Additionally, he is a five-star rated speech writer on Fiverr. He has written speeches for keynote speakers, business leaders, entrepreneurs, and politicians across the United States and around the world, including Australia, Belgium, Canada, France, Germany, Guyana, India, Indonesia, Israel, New Zealand, Singapore, and the United Arab Emirates.

He is the host of his own podcast, *Bruce Hurwitz Presents*, which has attracted guests and listeners from across the United States and as far away as England and Sweden, Australia and New Zealand.

Hurwitz is a nationally and internationally recognized authority on career and employment issues, having been cited in over 700 articles, appearing in more than 500 publications, including *The Wall Street Journal*, *USA Today*, and *US World and News Report,* throughout the United States and in some 30 foreign countries.

His social media network includes some 43,000 individuals. A frequent writer on LinkedIn, his articles have been read well over 400,000 times and have garnered national and international attention. He has been interviewed on the local New York Fox affiliate, Headline News and Fox Business Network.

A former member of the Board of Directors of the Manhattan Chamber of Commerce and founding producer and host of their weekly podcast, *The Voice of Manhattan Business*, since 2017 he has been a judge for the New York Public Library's annual business plan competition.

The author of well over 125 peer-reviewed books, articles and newspaper contributions, on topics ranging from International Relations and International Law to the use of technology to conducting an effective job search and having a successful career, his latest book, *The 21st Century Job Search*, published earlier this year, was an Amazon Number One best seller and Number One new release in multiple categories.

Made in the USA
Columbia, SC
20 March 2020